TEACH... ...H GAMES

TEACH... ...G
PROGRAMMING
CONCEPTS
THROUGH PLAY

CHRISTOPHER HARRIS AND PATRICIA HARRIS, Ph.D., WITH BRIAN MAYER

Rosen
Classroom
PROFESSIONAL RESOURCES™

Published in 2015 by The Rosen Publishing Group, Inc.
29 East 21st Street, New York, NY 10010

First Edition

Cataloging-in-Publication Data

Harris, Christopher.
Teaching programming concepts through play/by Christopher Harris, Patricia Harris, PhD, and Brian Mayer.
p. cm. — (Teaching through games)
Includes appendix.
ISBN 978-1-4994-9012-1 (paperback)
1. Computer programming — Study and teaching. 2. Computer science — Study and teaching (Middle school) — Activity programs. 3. Teaching — Aids and devices. I. Harris, Christopher, 1977-. II. Harris, Patricia. III. Mayer, Brian. IV. Title.
QA76.27 H37 2015
004.07—d23

Manufactured in the United States of America

Code Word: thinksmart

Use the code word above to register for an account on the series website at http://teachingthroughgames.com. Or, if you have already registered, use the code to add this book to your existing account. The website contains the readings and sheets referenced in this book as well as additional game elements. There is also a discussion forum where you can share successful practices and ask questions.

Photo Credits: cover (image & background) © Pablo Blazquez Dominguez/Getty Images; cover (wire), pp. i, 72 © klenger/pp. iv © Universal Images Group/Getty Images; p. vii © www.alltpaettkort.se/produkt/ricochet-robots.

CONTENTS

INTRODUCTION

Computers are not smart. Sure, they can do complex math faster than the blink of an eye, and the Internet seems to know just about everything, but computers by themselves are not smart. Computers can only do what the programs they run tell them to do. Even the most advanced artificial intelligence and learning computers are still restricted by the code that a human wrote. For now at least.

COMPUTER PROGRAMMING

Writing computer programs, like playing a game, is all about rules. Computer programs must be written using a very specific vocabulary and punctuation style. Some of the most annoying bugs—errors in computer programs, named for an actual moth that disrupted an early computer—can happen when a programmer forgets to add a semicolon or other bit of punctuation. There is a specific process and procedure for writing a computer program, just like there is a process to playing a game. To be successful, you have to work within the process. This high level of similarity makes writing computer games a great way to learn programming.

In this guide, though, we aren't going to talk about the actual writing of computer code. Learning a programming language is not hard; what is hard is developing the proper mind-set that allows one to think like a computer. The nuances of proper syntax and punctuation unique to each language will be mastered through practice and fixing lots of bugs. A deeper understanding of how computer programs work and the underlying flow of logic and processes within code is a much more effective starting point. This resourse will present four analog games that build that solid foundation. The games introduce some of the intellectual concepts required for learning computer programming regardless of the actual language involved.

The problem with jumping right in to actual code is that one's thinking is then restricted to the bits of code already mastered. Our ability to envision new possibilities is limited by the existing schema in our minds for computer programming. Jean Piaget's educational theories propose that our minds use schemata to organize prior knowledge and understandings about objects and experiences. New learning has to be fitted into an existing schema, so a broader base schema is more ready to assimilate and accommodate new learning. In other words, by first learning how computers think and how computer programs work, students are better prepared to learn the specifics of individual languages. They will already have schemata for different ideas, like conditional statements and Boolean logic, based on the exercises here, so when it comes time to learn that a language handles conditionals using a switch or case statement, there already exists a deeper understanding of the concept upon which to now attach a new label.

ABEUNT STUDIA IN MORES

This quote from Ovid's *Heroides* is generally translated as meaning studies/pursuits become habits or part of ones character. George Boole used the quote at the end of his introduction to what would become one of the most important texts in computer science, *The Mathematical Analysis of Logic*, written in 1847. Boole uses the quote to defend the learning of match and sciences. It is included here to reinforce the proposition for preparing students for learning code by teaching them to think in a computer programming mindset. This book will present studies and games that will help students internalize the computer programming mind-set; logical thinking, consideration of conditional statements, use of variables, and other ways of thinking like a computer will become habits of the mind. The mind itself will then be ready to learn the actual writing of computer code.

Consider, for example, the classic introduction snippet of code for printing "hello world." At the conclusion of the lessons in this guide, successful students will be able to think about this briefest of programs in a new light. They should be able to propose ways to use variables to learn a name and then write out "hello <name>." Having learned about conditional statements, they should be able to propose a check for the time of day to have the code print out "good morning <name>" or "good evening <name>" depending on the time run.

Students don't have to know how to write this code, just that this code is possible. Knowing that something is possible and being able to imagine it, describe it, and even think about how it would interact with the world—these are the critical first steps. Thinking this way demonstrates true computer fluency.

LET'S PLAY A GAME

In the first section, we will introduce the very basic concepts of how computers process information. The focus will be on having students understand the concepts of the binary system and the constant push for efficiency within computer work. Ricochet Robots, though perhaps more of a puzzle than a game, provides a wonderful playground for exploring these concepts. Customized variations for gameplay give students an initial experience of giving commands to a computer.

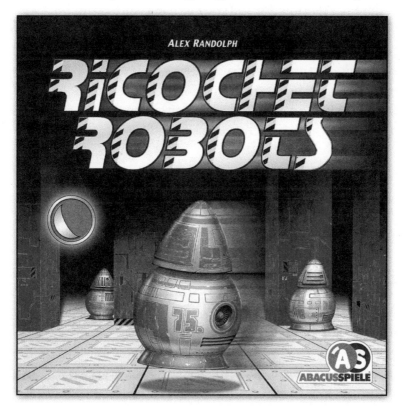

RoboRally, a crazy fun game of driving robots through an industrial maze, is used in the second section to talk about different styles of computer programming. In the first games, students will use a non-structured method of programming for their robots similar to initial code in the BASIC language. In custom variations developed for this guide, further experiences with the game will have students use structured programming with repeatable methods, or blocks of code. At the end, we will also explore the much more common modern style of object-oriented code.

For chapter 3, we will use Old Town to explore Boolean logic. This game can be difficult to find, but if it is possible to access a copy it is an amazing learning experience. Students will use the game to think about how Boolean operators like AND, OR, and NOT (as well as more advanced operators like XOR or NAND) limit and expand sets of information.

In the final section, we will start writing a program. This will be an analog program, though, written within the Parsely Game System as code for a human and not a computer. The Parsely System is a method of writing interactive fiction, or text adventure games. This culminating experience will have students using all of the knowledge they have gained to think like a computer and write increasingly complex interactive code for their peers to execute.

NEXT STEPS

If students are eager to begin exploring actual computer code at the end of this resourse, I highly recommend following up the work on interactive fiction presented in chapter 4 with work on Inform 7. This free program provides a powerful framework for writing and playing interactive text games. The code is written in a very natural way using regular English structure but with words that have special meanings in Inform 7. For example, to create a room, one simply writes: "The Living Room is a room." The program understands that the word "is" means that something is being created with certain properties; in this case we are telling Inform that the something is a room. Inform then knows that rooms have names, and so looks to the first part of the sentence before the command "is" to find the name. The writing flows very naturally, especially after experiences writing and playing games using the Parsely System.

Another great option is to look at a visual block system of coding like MIT's Scratch or Google's Blocky. Both of these languages have code snippets and operations presented on puzzle pieces that the coder snaps together as needed. This means that users are thinking about the program at a conceptual level and not worrying about syntax and punctuation. A nice extension that mirrors the approach taken here.

GAME 1:
RICOCHET ROBOTS

What does it mean to think like a computer? Really, we want to think like a computer programmer. But as with learning any new language, the real desire is fluency. An indicator of true language fluency is the ability to think in the new language as opposed to thinking in a first language and then translating in your head. To really master computer programming then, one must start to think like a computer.

TECHNICALLY SPEAKING

How Computers Think

Computers and computer programming crave efficiency. As the first computer programs were being written in the 1940s, efficiency was an absolute requirement as the computers were incredibly primitive. At this point in history, computers were as much mechanical as electronic. They used paper tape or punch cards for input and output; the first computer monitors were still decades in the future.

Through the 1960s, programs were written in assembly language, the lowest possible level of programming that delivers each instruction to the computer in binary form. Binary—a numerical base consisting of just two elements, 1 and 0—is how computers really think. At the foundational level of thinking in computers, things are either on (1) or off (0); there is no maybe. There is also no ambiguity.

Even though modern computers have enough resources to compensate for inefficient programs, efficiency is still a hallmark of a well-written program. A poorly designed element of a web page may only add a few hundred milliseconds to the load time for the page, but when there are hundreds of elements on each page it can add up. Poorly written code on websites can create noticeable wait times as each page loads and cause visitors to go to a different site out of frustration. If you were designing a website for a store, this could mean lost business. Computer games with inefficient code and long wait times for loading new levels are also very frustrating. As games become more graphical, they must be written in a very efficient code that can handle the complex graphical data.

THE QUEST FOR EFFICIENCY

We can see the quest for efficiency in computer programming mirrored in Ricochet Robots. In this game—actually more of a puzzle—players seek the most efficient solution to a problem. Robots can be given a single command to move in a given direction, a move they will carry out until they run into something that stops them. Visualizing the board in their minds, players have to figure out the best set of commands to have a robot reach the goal in the fewest possible moves.

Ricochet Robots is reminiscent of an old computer challenge, the travelling salesman problem. Imagine a travelling salesman who needs to visit different cities to hawk his wares. What is the most efficient path that lets him visit all of the cities once, and only once, in the least amount of time? This is an incredibly hard math problem, something that computers are very good at. For the computer to solve the problem, though, someone has to write a computer program that tells the computer how to solve the problem. It wasn't until the 1990s that a team created the Concorde software that could handle the complex math involved. Unlike previous solutions that used the computer to check solutions or solve the math, this software actively sought out new solutions.

COMPUTERS AS PROBLEM SOLVERS

What makes computers so good at solving problems like this is that they can try every possible permutation in a very short time. Our brains are much slower, but this is what we are challenged to do in Ricochet Robots; consider every possible path and every possible move and find the most efficient way to get a robot to the goal. In computer programs, we have a number of ways to work through lists of possibilities. This is called conditional programming.

At the most basic level of selecting between a list of two possible choices, where something either is or is not true, computer programs use a method known as if-then. If-then statements are written in such a way as to test whether or not something is true and, if it is true, the method provides a then statement that can be executed. For example: if it is raining then open your umbrella. There are two possibilities, either it is raining or it isn't raining. If it is raining, the then statement should be executed, otherwise nothing happens. The if-then statement is a very powerful tool. It lets computer programs interact with the world as opposed to just executing an established routine.

The difference would be similar to the difference between passively watching a movie and actively participating as an audience member in improvisational comedy. The movie is established, and no matter how the audience responds—even if the audience starts getting up and walking out—it doesn't change and the movie keeps playing. Improv comedy, however, is interactive. The comedy troupe has some established programming, but there are also points for audience input. The information shouted out by the audience serves the same role as variables in programming. Improv teams have to then use conditional programing as they act out the scene, responding as new items are introduced or modified.

At a slightly higher level, we can use an if-then(-else) statement to assign a second possibility for an action to be executed in the case that the if statement is false. For even longer lists, we could just continue to write if-then statements. For example: if the stoplight is green, go; if the stoplight is yellow, prepare to stop; if the stoplight is red, stop. This, however, is rather inefficient as we are checking three if-then statements when only one can be true at any time. More advanced conditional programming methods use case or switch methods to handle larger lists of possibilities. These are the same, but different languages use different names for them. Case or switch methods establish a list of possibilities and reactions establishing a case for each situation. Other languages allow pattern-matching methods that would check the color of the stoplight with the intended reaction. These advanced methods are much more efficient.

PRACTICING COMPUTER THINKING

Being able to rationalize and process if-then(-else) statements or come up with more advanced conditional programming methods to apply to real-life situations is a great way to start thinking like a computer programmer and a computer. It is also important to have a clear understanding that computers use binary—a system consisting of only 1 and 0, on and off—as their foundation for programming. Finally, computers and computer programming thrive on efficiency. Conditional programming such as if-then statements and the logical interaction between inputs will be explored further in the next two sections.

For now, though, all of the concepts introduced here can be seen in Ricochet Robots. We have to think through all of the possibilities, or conditions, and then select the most efficient way to help the robot reach the goal. We cannot make partial moves, though. When a robot is switched on to move in a direction, it will continue moving in that direction until it hits a wall or another robot and switches to off. In the two lessons, we will explore finding efficient solutions both in the game and in real-life situations.

LESSON PLAN 1A

ESSENTIAL QUESTION

Why must computer programs be efficient?

VOCABULARY

The following vocabulary words are important concepts for the content of this lesson.

- Efficiency
- Binary
- Analytical engine
- Difference engine
- Charles Babbage
- Ada, Countess Lovelace

SUGGESTED READING RESOURCES

Primary Source Document
Excerpt from Note A of Ada Lovelace's translation of *Sketch of The Analytical Engine Invented by Charles Babbage*, originally written by L. F. Menabrea, 1842. This document is included after the lesson in an annotated form with vocabulary underlined and some important passages for close reading highlighted; it is available online at www.teachingthroughgames.com for printing.

Other Sources
Getting to Know the Raspberry Pi
Written by Nicki Peter Petrikowski
Published by Rosen Publishing, 2014
ISBN: 978147777709

Getting to Know Arduino
Written by Heather Moore Niver
Published by Rosen Publishing, 2014
ISBN: 9781477774991

MINI READING LESSON

While you are reading the available text material or the suggested reading resources, attempt to answer the following question: How do computers work and solve problems? Introduce the vocabulary words listed previously. They can be introduced even if they are not in the specific reading you have chosen.

It is important to note that Ada, Countess of Lovelace, is considered to be the first computer programmer based on the notes she added to *Sketch of The Analytical Engine Invented by Charles Babbage*. Sharing that the first computer programmer was a woman can help young women first learning about computers feel more confident in entering the field.

GUIDED PRACTICE

The teacher should introduce the playing of the Ricochet Robots using the side of the gameboard without diagonal lines and letting the students know that they must visualize the game board and decide, before any plays are made, an efficient way to move their robot. In this game, efficiency is what wins points, not just getting to the desired object but doing so in the fewest possible moves. It may help to demonstrate some scenarios showing exactly how robots move in the game. Given the way that the game works, a single game board can be set up for whole class use.

Play and Discuss

Have students reread each section of the text and discuss the following:
- Ada Lovelace wrote her notes in 1842, and yet was speaking about progamming computing engines using punch cards and repeatable code.
- How is finding a solution within Ricochet Robots similar to programming a computer?

- What are some strategies for finding more efficient paths within Ricochet Robots?

MODEL

To support students playing the game for the first time, it will help to provide a structured method for recording moves during the visualization phase. In the appendix, there is a planning sheet that students can use to map movements in a numbered way to keep track of their proposed solution. The order of movement can be especially critical if other robots are being moved into positions to serve as walls to end movement of the primary robot. Moving a blocker robot into the path too soon could result in robots ending up out of place rendering the solution unusable. Warn students to be careful of bugs in their programs! When bugs are found, make sure that students have a chance to debug and retest a modified solution. Ricochet Robots works better as a puzzle to master as opposed to a competitive game.

INDEPENDENT PRACTICE

Remind students of the vocabulary introduced for their reading and ask them to attempt to include that vocabulary in appropriate ways in the writing activities they do.

Writing Activities

Inform or Explain: Explain your method for solving a problem in Ricochet Robots. Engage in meta-thinking to figure out the exact steps taking place in your brain as you plan moves for the robots.

Express an Opinion: Why might computer programming be compared to playing a game? Explain why you agree or disagree using evidence from your experiences in Ricochet Robots and in other games you have played.

Sharing/Reflection

Have individuals or groups share and discuss their work with the class.

Assessment

Collect completed formative assessment (activity for model section) and writing activities and review. As was noted in the model section, the goal for the planning sheet in this initial playthrough of the game is evidence of mastery. Students should be expected to debug their solution until they find one that works. In the explain piece, students might find meta-thinking a challenge. It may help to have them work out a new puzzle with a partner, talking aloud about everything they are thinking. Answers will vary greatly in the opinion piece, but writing should include evidence that defends the position taken.

Extension Activities

Further Play: Have students play another game of Ricochet Robots using the sides of the boards that include the angled barriers and the rules for how they work.

Further Research: Have students research the issue of web page load time. Why is this an issue, both from a technical and an economic view? Why has the problem of slow load times been getting worse?

NOTE A OF ADA LOVELACE'S TRANSLATION ON ANALYTICAL ENGINE

Excerpt from Note A of Ada Lovelace's translation of *Sketch of The Analytical Engine Invented by Charles Babbage*, originally written by L. F. Menabrea, 1842.

Those who view **mathematical science, not merely as a vast body** of abstract and <u>immutable truths</u>, whose intrinsic beauty, symmetry and logical completeness, when regarded in their connexion together as a whole, entitle them to a prominent place in the interest of all profound and logical minds, but as possessing a yet deeper interest for the human race, when it is remembered that this science constitutes the language through which alone we can adequately express the great facts of the natural world, and those unceasing changes of mutual relationship which, visibly or invisibly, consciously or unconsciously to our immediate physical perceptions, are interminably going on in the agencies of the creation we live amidst: those who thus think on mathematical truth as the instrument through which the weak mind of man can most effectually read his Creator's works, will regard with especial interest all that can tend to facilitate the translation of its principles into explicit practical forms.

The distinctive characteristic of the <u>Analytical Engine</u>, and that which has rendered it possible to endow mechanism with such extensive faculties as bid fair to make this engine the executive right-hand of abstract algebra, is the introduction into it of the principle which Jacquard devised for regulating, by means of <u>punched cards</u>, the most complicated patterns in the fabrication of brocaded stuffs. It is in this that the distinction between the two engines lies. Nothing of the sort exists in the <u>Difference Engine</u>. We may say most aptly, that the Analytical Engine weaves algebraical patterns just as the <u>Jacquard-loom</u> weaves flowers and leaves. Here, it seems to us, resides much more of originality than the Difference Engine can be fairly entitled to claim. We do not wish to deny to this latter all such claims. **We believe that it is the only proposal or attempt ever made to construct a calculating machine founded on the principle of successive orders of differences, and capable of printing off its own results; and that this engine surpasses its predecessors, both in the extent of the calculations which it can perform, in the facility, certainty and accuracy with which it can effect them, and in the absence of all necessity for the intervention of human intelligence during the performance of its calculations.** Its nature is, however, limited to the strictly arithmetical, and it is far from being the first or only scheme for constructing arithmetical calculating machines with more or less of success.

The bounds of arithmetic were however outstepped the moment the idea of applying the cards had occurred; and the Analytical Engine does not occupy common ground with mere "calculating machines." It holds a position wholly its own; and the considerations it suggests are most interesting in their nature. **In enabling mechanism to combine together general symbols in successions of unlimited variety and extent, a uniting link is established between the operations of matter and the abstract mental processes of the most abstract branch of mathematical science.** A new, a vast, and a powerful language is developed for the future use of analysis, in which to wield its truths so that these may become of more speedy and accurate practical application for the purposes of mankind than the means hitherto in our possession have rendered possible. Thus not only the mental and the material, but the theoretical and the practical in the mathematical world, are brought into more intimate and effective connexion with each other. We are not aware of its being on record that anything partaking in the nature of what is so well designated the Analytical Engine has been hitherto proposed, or even thought of, as a practical possibility, any more than the idea of a thinking or of a reasoning machine.

We will touch on another point which constitutes an important distinction in the modes of operating of the Difference and Analytical Engines. In order to enable the former to do its business, it is necessary to put into its columns the series of numbers constituting the first terms of the several orders of differences for whatever is the particular table under consideration. The machine then works upon these as its data. But these data must themselves have been already computed through a series of calculations by a human head. **Therefore that engine can only produce results depending on data which have been arrived at by the explicit and actual working out of processes that are in their nature different from any that come within the sphere of its own powers. In other words, an** analysing process must have been gone through by a human mind in order to obtain the data upon which the engine then synthetically builds its results. The Difference Engine is in its character exclusively synthetical, while the Analytical Engine is equally capable of <u>analysis or of synthesis</u>.

It is true that the Difference Engine can calculate to a much greater extent with these few preliminary data, than the data themselves required for their own determination. The table of squares, for instance, can be calculated to any extent whatever, when the numbers one and two are furnished; and a very few differences computed at any part of a table of logarithms would enable the engine to calculate many hundreds or even thousands of logarithms. Still the circumstance of its requiring, as a previous condition, that any function whatever shall have been numerically worked out, makes it very inferior in its nature and advantages to an engine which, like the Analytical Engine, requires merely that we should know the succession and distribution of the operations to be performed; without there being any occasion, in order to obtain data on which it can work, for our ever having gone through either the same particular operations which it is itself to effect, or any others. Numerical data must of course be given it, but they are mere arbitrary ones; not data that could only be arrived at through a systematic and necessary series of previous numerical calculations, which is quite a different thing.

To this it may be replied, that an analysing process must equally have been performed in order to furnish the Analytical Engine with the necessary operative data; and that herein may also lie a possible source of error. Granted that the actual mechanism is unerring in its processes, the cards may give it wrong orders. This is unquestionably the case; but there is much less chance of error, and likewise far less expenditure of time and labour, where operations only, and the distribution of these operations, have to be made out, than where explicit numerical results are to be attained. In the case of the Analytical Engine we have undoubtedly to lay out a certain capital of analytical labour in one particular line; but this is in order that the engine may bring us in a much larger return in another line. **It should be remembered also that the cards, when once made out for any formula, have all the generality of algebra, and include an infinite number of particular cases.**

We have dwelt considerably on the distinctive peculiarities of each of these engines, because we think it essential to place their respective attributes in strong relief before the apprehension of the public; and to define with clearness and accuracy the wholly different nature of the principles on which each is based, so as to make it self-evident to the reader (the mathematical reader at least) in what manner and degree the powers of the Analytical Engine transcend those of an engine, which, like the Difference Engine, can only work out such results as may be derived from one restricted and particular series of processes, such as those included in $\triangle^n U_2 = 0$. We think this of importance, because we know that there exists considerable vagueness and inaccuracy in the mind of persons in general on the subject. There is a misty notion amongst most of those who have attended at all to it, that two "calculating machines" have been successively invented by the same person within the last few years; while others again have never heard but of the one original "calculating machine," and are not aware of there being any extension upon this. For either of these two classes of persons the above considerations are appropriate. While the latter require a knowledge of the fact that there are two such inventions, the former are not less in want of accurate and well-defined information on the subject. No very clear or correct ideas prevail as to the characteristics of each engine, or their respective advantages or disadvantages; and in meeting with those incidental allusions, of a more or less direct kind, which occur in so many publications of the day, to these machines, it must frequently be matter of doubt which "calculating machine" is referred to, or whether both are included in the general allusion.

We are desirous likewise of removing two misapprehensions which we know obtain, to some extent, respecting these engines. In the first place it is very generally supposed that the Difference Engine, after it had been completed up to a certain point, suggested the idea of the Analytical Engine; and that the second is in fact the improved offspring of the first, and grew out of the existence of its predecessor, through some natural or else accidental combination of ideas suggested by this one. **Such a supposition is in this instance contrary to the facts; although it seems to be almost an obvious inference, wherever two inventions, similar in their nature and objects, succeed each other closely in order of time, and strikingly in order of value; more especially when the same individual is the author of both. Nevertheless the ideas which led to the Analytical Engine occurred in a manner wholly independent of any that were connected with the Difference Engine.** These ideas are indeed in their own intrinsic nature independent of the latter engine, and might equally have occurred had it never existed nor been even thought of at all.

The second of the misapprehensions above alluded to relates to the well-known suspension, during some years past, of all progress in the construction of the Difference Engine. Respecting the circumstances which have interfered with the actual completion of either invention, we offer no opinion; and in fact are not possessed of the data for doing so, had we the inclination. **But we know that some persons suppose these obstacles (be they what they may) to have arisen in consequence of the subsequent invention of the Analytical Engine while the former was in progress. We have ourselves heard it even lamented that an idea should ever have occurred at all, which had turned out to be merely the means of arresting what was already in a course of successful execution, without substituting the superior invention in its stead. This notion we can contradict in the most unqualified manner. The progress of the Difference Engine had long been suspended, before there were even the least crude glimmerings of any invention superior to it.** Such glimmerings, therefore, and their subsequent development, were in no way the original cause of that suspension; although, where difficulties of some kind or other evidently already existed, it was not perhaps calculated to remove or lessen them that an invention should have been meanwhile thought of, which, while including all that the first was capable of, possesses powers so extended as to eclipse it altogether.

We leave it for the decision of each individual (after he has possessed himself of competent information as to the characteristics of each engine) to determine how far it ought to be matter of regret that such an accession has been made to the powers of human science, even if it has (which we greatly doubt) increased to a certain limited extent some already existing difficulties that had arisen in the way of completing a valuable but lesser work. We leave it for each to satisfy himself as to the wisdom of desiring the obliteration (were that now possible) of all records of the more perfect invention, in order that the comparatively limited one might be finished. The Difference Engine would doubtless fulfil all those practical objects which it was originally destined for. It would certainly calculate all the tables that are more directly necessary for the physical purposes of life, such as nautical and other computations. Those who incline to very strictly utilitarian views may perhaps feel that the peculiar powers of the Analytical Engine bear upon questions of abstract and speculative science, rather than upon those involving every-day and ordinary human interests. These persons being likely to possess but little sympathy, or possibly acquaintance, with any branches of science which they do not find to be useful (according to their definition of that word), may conceive that the undertaking of that engine, now that the other one is already in progress, would be a barren and unproductive laying out of yet more money and labour; in fact, a work of supererogation. Even in the utilitarian aspect, however, we do not doubt that very valuable practical results would be developed by the extended faculties of the Analytical Engine; some of which results we think we could now hint at, had we the space; and others, which it may not yet be possible to foresee, but which would be brought forth by the daily increasing requirements of science, and by a more intimate practical acquaintance with the powers of the engine, were it in actual existence.

On general grounds, both of an a priori description as well as those founded on the scientific history and experience of mankind, we see strong presumptions that such would be the case. Nevertheless all will probably concur in feeling that the completion of the Difference Engine would be far preferable to the non-completion of any calculating engine at all. With whomsoever or wheresoever may rest the present causes of difficulty that apparently exist towards either the completion of the old engine, or the commencement of the new one, we trust they will not ultimately result in this generation's being acquainted with these inventions through the medium of pen, ink and paper merely; and still more do we hope, that for the honour of our country's reputation in the future pages of history, these causes will not lead to the completion of the undertaking by some other nation or government. This could not but be matter of just regret; and equally so, whether the obstacles may have originated in private interests and feelings, in considerations of a more public description, or in causes combining the nature of both such solutions.

We refer the reader to the 'Edinburgh Review' of July 1834, for a very able account of the Difference Engine. The writer of the article we allude to has selected as his prominent matter for exposition, a wholly different view of the subject from that which M. Menabrea has chosen. The former chiefly treats it under its mechanical aspect, entering but slightly into the mathematical principles of which that engine is the representative, but giving, in considerable length, many details of the mechanism and contrivances by means of which it tabulates the various orders of differences. M. Menabrea, on the contrary, exclusively develops the analytical view; taking it for granted that mechanism is able to perform certain processes, but without attempting to explain how; and devoting his whole attention to explanations and illustrations of the manner in which analytical laws can be so arranged and combined as to bring every branch of that vast subject within the grasp of the assumed powers of mechanism. It is obvious that, in the invention of a calculating engine, these two branches of the subject are equally essential fields of investigation, and that on their mutual adjustment, one to the other, must depend all success. They must be made to meet each other, so that the weak points in the powers of either department may be compensated by the strong points in those of the other. They are indissolubly connected, though so different in their intrinsic nature, that perhaps the same mind might not be likely to prove equally profound or successful in both. We know those who doubt whether the powers of mechanism will in practice prove adequate in all respects to the demands made upon them in the working of such complicated trains of machinery as those of the above engines, and who apprehend that unforeseen practical difficulties and disturbances will arise in the way of accuracy and of facility of operation. The Difference Engine, however, appears to us to be in a great measure an answer to these doubts. It is complete as far as it goes, and it does work with all the anticipated success. The Analytical Engine, far from being more complicated, will in many respects be of simpler construction; and it is a remarkable circumstance attending it, that with very simplified means it is so much more powerful.

The article in the 'Edinburgh Review' was written some time previous to the occurrence of any ideas such as afterwards led to the invention of the Analytical Engine; and in the nature of the Difference Engine there is much less that would invite a writer to take exclusively, or even prominently, the mathematical view of it, than in that of the Analytical Engine; although mechanism has undoubtedly gone much further to meet mathematics, in the case of this engine, than of the former one. Some publication embracing the mechanical view of the Analytical Engine is a desideratum which we trust will be supplied before long.

LESSON PLAN 1B

ESSENTIAL QUESTION

Why must a programmer give explicit directions to a computer?

VOCABULARY

The following vocabulary words are important concepts for the content of this lesson.

- Explicit directions
- Conditional programming
- If-then
- If-then(-else)
- Permutations

Suggested Reading Resources

Getting to Know Ruby
Written by Heather Moore Niver
Published by Rosen Publishing, 2014
ISBN: 9781477777138

Getting to Know Python
Written by Simone Payment
Published by Rosen Publishing, 2014
ISBN: 9781477777176

Mini Reading Lesson

While you are reading the available text material or the suggested reading resources, attempt to answer the following question: How much are we taking for granted when we give someone directions? Introduce the previous vocabulary words. They can be introduced even if they are not in the specific reading you have chosen.

Guided Practice

To demonstrate the importance of explicit directions in a computer program, you as the teacher are going to make a peanut butter and jelly sandwich. Instead of using your established knowledge about making a PBJ, however, you will follow the exact directions provided by the students. Start by having the materials in front of you and then ask students for the first three steps to making the sandwich. Follow them explicitly! If the students say spread the peanut butter on the bread, either take the jar of peanut butter and pass it along the bag of bread, or get out a glob of peanut butter and spread that over the bread bag. Messy, but it makes the point that explicit directions are critical for programming.

Start again, and prompt the students to think about each explicit step that must be taken. Ordering of steps is important. It will also be important for students to establish some if-then statements. For example, most people align the two pieces of bread in the same direction when forming the sandwich, but an explicit program will have to include an if-then check to see if rotation is needed. You may need to coach students to think about if-then situations.

Participate and Discuss

Have students think about the sandwich exercise and reflect on the following questions:

- Why did the students initially fail to include explicit directions?
- Why is giving explicit instructions at this level of detail so uncomfortable for most people?
- How did the demonstration relate to design of a computer program?
- How many if-then situations do we resolve on a daily basis without even thinking about them?

MODEL

Play through Ricochet Robots using a variant ruleset that focuses on explicit directions. Students will use the same planning sheet to record their moves, but this time they can provide explicit directions such as number of steps to move for some of the robots. In this variant we will use the silver robot as the primary robot that moves as normal, ricocheting off of walls and the other robots, to reach the target. The four colored robots can be given explicit instructions to move them into exact positions to serve as walls. Instructions will include a direction of movement and the number of spaces to move for any or all of the four robots. For scoring, count the number of instructions given to any of the four colored robots as well as the silver robot. Then, check other permutations—possible sets of moves—to see if a more efficient solution can be found.

INDEPENDENT PRACTICE

Remind students of the vocabulary introduced for their reading and ask them to attempt to include that vocabulary in appropriate ways in the writing activities they do.

Writing Activities

Narrative: Think about what might happen when a friend gives you directions to a new restaurant that are not explicit enough. Write a text message conversation between you and your friend with at least twenty short messages seeking clarification on the directions.

Inform or Explain: Write explicit directions for getting dressed in the morning. Include if-then statements as needed to ensure that the person following the directions is wearing appropriate clothing.

Express an Opinion: Should you always give people explicit directions? Why or why not?

SHARING/REFLECTION

Have individuals or groups share and discuss their work with the class.

ASSESSMENT

Collect completed formative assessment (activity for model section) and writing activities and review. The planning sheet for the model section should demonstrate attempts to find more efficient solutions to solve the game puzzle. Demonstrated effort toward efficiency is more important here than students actually finding the most efficient solution (though that is a laudable goal as well). In the narrative piece, the conversation should reflect seeking clarification with specific directions. For the explain piece, students should provide very explicit, step-by-step directions. If-then statements might include checking if it is a school day or not, or what the weather might be and whether the clothes are clean. For the opinion piece answers will vary greatly. A successful opinion, though, should consider ideas such as the presence of shared understandings in a community that fill in for explicit directions most of the time.

Extension Activities

Further Research: Research how different computer languages handle conditional programming. If-then statements are just the beginning. Explore how case/switch statements, pattern matching, and other ways to compare two or more possibilities are handled in programs.

GAME 2: ROBORALLY

RoboRally (Wizards of the Coast, 2005) has players giving their robots commands to race through an industrial maze in an attempt to be the first to reach a goal. Just as there are many different ways to program your robot to reach the finish line in RoboRally, there are many different ways to program a computer. You can explore the many different varieties of programming languages with a bit of research; we are going to focus here on two primary families of languages.

TECHNICALLY SPEAKING

As we learned in the last section, the first computer programs were "written" in holes on paper tape and punch cards. Even as the first coded languages emerged, they were written as assembly code at the most basic level of binary input. These languages developed over time, but they still remained rather primitive compared to modern code. The key distinction is that the earlier languages used non-structured code—the code was written in a linear form with numbered lines that the computer, for the most part, stepped through sequentially. In contrast, the large majority of modern programming languages are structured; that is, they use a structure of functions or methods that are called as a block to execute portions of the program.

NON-STRUCTURED PROGRAMMING

The most famous of the non-structured programming languages is BASIC. This was actually a whole family of languages, but all of them shared the common acronym for Beginner's All-purpose Symbolic Instruction Code. The first BASIC language was developed in 1964, but one flavor of BASIC, Microsoft's Visual Basic, is still used today.

BASIC was developed as a way to bring computer programming to more people. By using a text-based language with easily remembered and interpreted commands, BASIC added a human-friendly layer on top of assembly code. The language understands basic commands and steps through lines of code in sequential order executing the commands as written. A very well known command in BASIC is PRINT as in PRINT "Hello, World!" which causes the computer terminal to display the phrase "Hello, World!" For many early computer users in the 1970s and 1980s, this was the first "program" they wrote. It was the first time they made a computer do what they told it to do. As a young child in the early 1980s who had this exact experience, I can assure you that the realization that you can use the computer as a tool, not just a toy, is a powerful feeling.

Even though it is referred to as a non-structured language, in BASIC each command is numbered, usually counting by 10s so that additional lines can be added in between if needed. The distinction of a program being structured or non-structured doesn't refer to simple things like line numbering, but rather to the use of advanced functions and subroutines. Though the numbered lines in BASIC seem to be structured, the word here is being used with a more technical definition. In BASIC, there is no real structure in the sense of being able to tell the computer to execute a full subroutine. Line numbering allowed the use of the infamous GO TO command that would tell the computer to jump to a specific line number. This could—and often did if programmers weren't very careful—create infinite loops as the program stepped through and then looped back with a GO TO. A basic block of programming could be executed in order by having the program loop back through the specific lines, but as we will see this is very different from what happens in a structured language.

STRUCTURED PROGRAMMING

In 1968, a Dutch computer scientist named Edsger Dijkstra submitted a letter titled "Go To Statement Considered Harmful" to the editors of *Communications of the ACM* (Association for Computing Machinery). "The go to statement as it stands is just too primitive," Dijkstra wrote, "it is too much an invitation to make a mess of one's program." Instead, he wanted programmers to use more explicit methods of repeating code blocks. The result was the development of a new set of structured languages that made use of subroutines to break out blocks of code as well as for and while loops to avoid the mess of using go to statements.

In a structured language like Pascal, developed in the 1970s, programmers could expand their writing to include many new capabilities. Pascal did a much better job handling variables—dynamic bits of data that are assigned to a variable placeholder. Pascal also used repeat until loops that would let a programmer specify the exact number of times to loop a command. By including a statement in the repeat until command block that added one to the value of a variable during each pass through of the command block, the computer could be told to repeat until the variable reached a certain value. Pascal also used case statements introduced in the first section as a more advanced way to handle complex groups of if-then statements.

OBJECT-ORIENTED PROGRAMMING

Many modern programming languages are a type of structured language referred to as object-oriented because they focus on the idea of an object made up of code and data. Consider, for example, an electronic construction sign on the side of a road. If that were an object in a program, we could talk about it as having code and data. The code, or behavior, might be to flash through three screens of messages. The messages themselves, the data, are also embedded into the object. By combining the code and data into a single object means we can easily change the properties of either—change the sign to display a single static message, or change the message itself—without having to change any code in the main program. One widely used object-oriented programming language is C++ (read aloud as C plus plus), which is used in many video games.

Object-oriented programming is built around the idea of objects represented through sections of code. Objects can fall into hierarchical classes so that there could be code applied to any object that is part of the vehicle class to describe how movement happens. The vehicle movement code might have inputs such as direction and speed and outputs defining the new location of the vehicle. Subclasses of vehicles will also be needed to handle differences in what are called instances. Instances are the implementations of class objects. For example, an instance of a car will have certain aspects that need to be programmed; the need for gas, the use of pedals and a steering wheel, and more. A horse and buggy is also a vehicle, but it needs very different specific code that checks for a horse in order to allow for movement. No matter what type of vehicle it is, though, some of the base code, such as movement, will be shared across the class. Object-oriented programming is built around making it very easy to utilize shared chunks of code called methods that describe how things work.

Programming Paradigms in Action

So what do these different methods, or paradigms, of programming look like in action? We can visualize them through variations of play in RoboRally. By default, RoboRally uses non-structured programming for the robots. Players lay out commands in a linear order with a single command per card. Cards are numbered like lines of code in non-structured programming, as a way to determine priority each turn with lower numbers executing first. As a variant, though, we can set up a variety of pre-defined functions that can be called by the robot to execute blocks of commands. For example, we could create a function that causes the robot to turn and then drive forward within a single command. By adding in variables for dynamic forward movement, we can create a situation where players now have to select both functions to call and a variable to pass specifying how much movement should take place. We can also create functions for different types of robots to create different instances of the class robot based on the special cards in the game. This starts to approximate object-oriented programming.

LESSON PLAN 2A

ESSENTIAL QUESTION

How can non-structured programs go wrong?

VOCABULARY

The following vocabulary words are important concepts for the content of this lesson.
- Non-structured programming
- Structured programming
- Line numbering

MINI READING LESSON

While you are talking about programming languages and working through the exercises, attempt to answer the following question: What are the limitations of non-structured programming languages? Introduce the vocabulary words above. They can be introduced even if they are not in the specific reading you have chosen.

GUIDED PRACTICE

To help students understand the mechanisms used in RoboRally, we are going to first make them take on the role of the robot. Have students stand up and then, using cards from the game, give them a series of directions to follow. When they bump into a wall the student will sit down. If they bump into another student (gently please), then that other student is pushed (metaphorically) one step in the direction of the first student's movement. This mirrors what will happen in the game. Complete eight to ten movements using cards.

Then, set up the game board and have students play three turns going through the five program registers for each robot on each turn. Ignore rules about laser damage for this round, but still account for movement along conveyer belts and bumping based on priority. Use the Risky Exchange map as described in the rulebook but only place the first target flag on the board.

Discuss

Considering the texts and the preceding activity, discuss the following:

- What role does chance play in RoboRally? Does chance factor in computer programming?
- What can go wrong in a non-structured program where steps are carried out sequentially with no checks for success?
- Why did Edsger Dijkstra write so negatively about go to statements?

Model

We are using this game as a teaching tool, so even though it is quite fun to watch robots bumping into each other and falling into pits, that is not the goal of our use. To remain focused on the instructional objective, have students plan out an ideal route from a starting point to each of the checkpoints on the Risky Exchange map. Students can use any of the available movement cards from the deck. Have students compare solutions to see which routes are more efficient. It will be important for students to still think about conveyer belt actions, even if they don't have to worry about lasers and being pushed by other robots.

Use the RoboRally planning sheet found in the appendix and available online at www.teachingthroughgames.com for printing for students to record their program. Step through the programs in small groups and then have students work to debug any issues that arise.

Students should write a reflective paragraph describing changes they would make in their program and why the changes would be needed.

INDEPENDENT PRACTICE

Remind students of the vocabulary introduced for their reading and ask them to attempt to include that vocabulary in appropriate ways in the writing activities they do.

Writing Activities

Narrative: From the perspective of a robot who spends its days riding conveyer belts and sometimes ending up in pits, send a memo to the boss explaining how you would improve the programming methods of the robot programmer causing you daily grief.

Inform or Explain: What are the limitations of non-structured programming?

Express an Opinion: Explore influential figures in the history of computer programming and identify five that you would propose as the founding members for a programming hall of fame. Defend your choices.

SHARING/REFLECTION

Have individuals or groups share and discuss their work with the class.

ASSESSMENT

Collect completed formative assessment (activity for model section) and writing activities and review. The RoboRally planning sheet should describe a successful program that accounts for the conveyer belts and other obstacles of the board. In the reflective paragraph, look for students to identify improvements or misunderstandings such as failure to account for the robot's perspective in defining turns. The narrative is meant to be a bit fun, but the writing should still talk about the need for debugging, trial runs, and other ways to avoid errors. In the inform piece, limitations might include the inability to gracefully exit a program midway, the problems of looping in go to statements, and the need to constantly re-write common code elements.

EXTENSION ACTIVITIES

Further Research: In BASIC, the go to statement has achieved a level of infamy rarely seen in computer programming. What was so bad about using go to?

Further Play: Play a game of RoboRally under the normal rule set. Have fun doing so.

LESSON PLAN 2B

ESSENTIAL QUESTION

What advantages do structured programming languages offer?

VOCABULARY

The following vocabulary words are important concepts for the content of this lesson.
- Structured programming
- Variable
- Function
- Method
- Object
- Class
- Instance

MINI READING LESSON

While you are talking about programming languages and working through the exercises, attempt to answer the following question:

What are the advantages of structured programming languages? Introduce the previous vocabulary words. They can be introduced even if they are not in the specific reading you have chosen.

GUIDED PRACTICE

One of the key ideas in structured programming is the creation of methods and functions; blocks of code that can be easily called for repeated use to complete simple tasks. In some languages these blocks are also called procedures. To help students understand how methods work, we can revisit the peanut butter sandwich exercise from section 1. Explain to the students that in creating a sandwich, there are a number of repeated actions. For example, both the peanut butter and the jelly are spread on the bread using a knife. In non-structured code, you have to write them out separately or risk getting stuck in an endless go to loop of spreading. In structured programming, though, you can define the action of spreading in a method, and then call the method while passing it the variable of the substance to be spread (either peanut butter or jelly).

Have students work in groups to identify five helpful methods that they would like to be able to use while playing RoboRally. The methods should be named with descriptive names and include the appropriate cards. Create cards to use in the game as a way to call the method to be implemented in place of a single card. In addition to naming the method, the group will need to define its priority number.

Share and Discuss

Have students share the methods they have created and discuss the following:

- How do methods help create more efficient code?
- How do methods help programmers reuse code?
- What is the importance of a method's name?
- How can passing variables to methods make them more useful?

- How can one of the methods created for RoboRally be improved by passing a variable?

Model

Have students play a game of RoboRally using one of the beginner courses defined in the book. In addition to the regular cards, players will also have access to a set of pre-defined methods to be substituted for one regular card. For this to work, each player will need to have a set of cards in hand that match the pre-defined methods created by the group in the Guided Practice section. The method cards remain in hand and return to the player's hand after use to be reused as needed. Each method can only be called once per turn. At the end of the game, each student should create a new method card that they would have wanted to use in the game. Explain the situations in which this method would be useful.

Independent Practice

Remind students of the vocabulary introduced for their reading and ask them to attempt to include that vocabulary in appropriate ways in the writing activities they do.

Writing Activities

Narrative: Assume the role of a game designer writing a computer game. What are three methods that your computer game will need? What are the names of the methods, what variables do they use, and what do they do?

Inform or Explain: Compare and contrast two types of structured languages. Pascal is a procedural language and C++ is an object-oriented language. How are they alike and different?

Express an Opinion: Is writing a method always an efficient use of programming time? Why or why not?

SHARING/REFLECTION

Have individuals or groups share and discuss their work with the class.

ASSESSMENT

Collect completed formative assessment (activity for model section) and writing activities and review. The additional method created at the end of the model section can do just about anything, but the student should be able to explain situations in which it would be useful. For the narrative, answers can again vary greatly, but the writing should demonstrate an understanding of methods and their importance in structured programming languages. The comparison of procedural languages and object-oriented languages starts to get very technical, but a general understanding should include the difference between the two. Of note will be the inclusion of objects within C++ and how objects allow programmers to clarify differences in a specific instance as part of a class.

EXTENSION ACTIVITIES

Further Research: Explore the characteristics of and code written in either Pascal and C++.

Further Play: Play a more advanced board in RoboRally with all of the rules for lasers and damage in place as well as the special options cards that add new powers to robots. Students can decide whether or not to use the special methods created in this lesson.

GAME 3: OLD TOWN

As was discussed in the first section, computers think in binary. Things are either 1 (on) or 0 (off), there is no middle ground. This is also true when looking at computer logic and answering questions. In fact, there is a whole field of math devoted to problems that can be answered as 1 or 0, true or false, called Boolean algebra. Old Town (Clicker Spiele) uses Boolean logic—a more common term for Boolean algebra in a computer programming context—to define the possible locations of different buildings during an archeological dig of an old Western town. Each time you play, the buildings will end up in different locations—the only possible locations that comply with the Boolean logic on the cards played that game.

TECHNICALLY SPEAKING

BOOLEAN LOGIC

In Boolean logic, we have a new set of operations. Addition, subtraction, and the other building blocks of numerical math are replaced by the basic Boolean operations of AND, OR, and NOT. In early days of Internet searching, these operations were very important. Searching is a resource intensive process; the computer makes it look easy, but really it is comparing what you type with every element in the database! Boolean operations helped narrow down the search to make it more efficient and better define your expected results. Exploring how Boolean operators work in computer searches can help us start to understand Boolean logic.

As an example of how the operations work, let us consider an Internet search looking for information about alligators and crocodiles. Knowing that they are technically different animals, we can use Boolean operators to manipulate our search results:

Alligators AND Crocodiles—Searching with the AND Boolean will return a restricted set of search results that must mention both alligators and crocodiles. These articles might help us compare the two animals as they are both mentioned in the same article.

Alligators OR Crocodiles—OR is the most expansive operator. Using this returns any article that mentions just alligators OR just crocodiles OR both alligators and crocodiles.

Alligators NOT Crocodiles—This search, or the reverse, will return articles that mention only the one animal. Articles just about the second animal, or about both animals, will be removed from the results.

Just like with regular mathematical operations, Boolean operators can be combined together to create a larger formula. For example, if we wanted to just read articles about either alligators or crocodiles but not both, we could use an extended Boolean query to set these limits. As with numerical algebra, we have to use parentheses to set apart sections of the query.

(Alligators OR Crocodiles) NOT (Alligators AND Crocodiles)—This query will consider the full set of articles about alligators OR crocodiles OR both, but then will exclude (NOT) the set of articles about alligators AND crocodiles. Therefore the results will only include articles that talk about just alligators or just crocodiles.

(Alligators NOT Crocodiles) AND (Crocodiles NOT Alligators)—As with any math, there are multiple ways to reach the same answer. This query will also provide the same set of results though it approaches the problem from a different direction. In this second example we are joining together two smaller sets of results whereas in the first example we removed a subset of results from a larger set.

Logic Gates

On a hardware level, computers all around us are programmed using Boolean logic embedded into electronic circuits called logic gates. You can play with these in Minecraft using redstone. Logic gates use Boolean logic to solve problems based on the flow of electricity. For example, in Minecraft you could build an AND gate with two levers and wires, each leading to one of two torches and then, through the AND gate, a power source. If the torches are connected with an AND gate, they will only light up when both switches are turned on to complete the AND circuit and provide connection to the power source. The basic logic gates match the basic operators in Boolean logic: AND, OR, and NOT. There are a few specialized logic gates that have been developed, however, to more efficiently address specific situations.

The NAND and NOR gates are a simple way to inverse (make NOT) the AND and OR gates. NAND, or NOT AND, is true only when the two inputs are both false. Having both inputs be true would be AND, anything else is NOT AND. The logical formula seen in the above example of limiting search results to just those that talk about either alligators or crocodiles but not both is used so much that there is a single logic gate called XOR, or exclusive OR. The XOR gate is only true when one of the two inputs is true, but not both or neither. There is also the opposite of this, the XNOR or exclusive NOT OR that is true when either both inputs are false or both inputs are true. Using this extended set of logic gates, you can start to program hardware with increasing complexity. In fact, these logical gates are the basis of the processors in the computer that handle the execution of code. This is why you can start to build a simple computer within Minecraft.

Thinking Logically

In Old Town, players have to adopt a very logical way of thinking in order to be successful. Like Twenty Questions, players in Old Town use deduction to slowly reduce false elements to reveal the final true element that remains. In Twenty Questions, the game basically just uses the NOT operation to provide a yes/no answer to simple questions. It must be noted, however, that twenty iterations of simple yes/no questions each carefully designed to eliminate half of the possible answers results in an astounding level of complexity. Mathematically, having twenty levels of 50/50 splits means we end up with 220 or 1,048,578 possibilities. Old Town uses much more complex logic.

There are three levels of cards in Old Town. The most basic cards, referred to as "4" cards for reasons that will become very obvious, establish four possible locations for a specific named building. Remember that Old Town has an empty town grid into which we are trying to place the different buildings based on information we find. The first information revealed might come from card 1 stating that the church was in sight of the cemetery. This limits the possible locations for the church to one of four building sites immediately surrounding the cemetery and so potential location markers are placed to record this information.

On a future turn, someone with the church building in front of them could play card 50 stating that my building—a variable that the player defines as the church in front of them waiting to be placed—was in the northern or southern outskirts of the town. This is an "8" card that establishes eight possible locations for a building but the building is variable. By playing this card, the player is in effect implementing an AND logic gate that combines the true elements of the first card as depicted on the game board and the new information from the card being played. Only two of the eight possible locations for the church depicted on card 50 match the information already established; that is only two of the locations pass the AND test. The two potential location markers that have now been determined false are removed and scored as points. The third level of cards, "8+8" cards, describe an AND or NOT situation for a named building and a variable for one of the player's buildings. These are powerful cards, but they can be difficult to play as the rules defined on the cards can quickly become impossible.

LESSON PLAN 3A

ESSENTIAL QUESTION

How do we limit and expand sets of information using Boolean logic?

VOCABULARY

The following vocabulary words are important concepts for the content of this lesson.
- Boolean logic
- Symbolic algebra
- AND
- OR
- NOT
- Set
- Limit
- Expand

SUGGESTED READING RESOURCES

Primary Source Document
Excerpt from the introduction of *The Mathematical Analysis of Logic* by George Boole, 1847. This document is included after the lesson in an annotated form with vocabulary underlined and some important passages for close reading highlighted; it is available online at www.teachingthroughgames.com for printing.

Other Sources
Conducting Basic and Advanced Searches
Written by Jason Porterfield
Published by Rosen Publishing, 2009
ISBN: 9781435853164

Digital and Information Literacy: New Research Techniques
Written by Ryan Randolph
Published by Rosen Publishing, 2011
ISBN: 9781448813216

MINI READING LESSON

While you are reading the available text material or the suggested reading resources, attempt to answer the following question: How do AND, OR, and NOT operations in Boolean logic limit and expand sets? Introduce the previous vocabulary words. They can be introduced even if they are not in the specific reading you have chosen.

Please note that the primary source document from George Boole, for whom Boolean operations are named, is a very complex text. In it, though, we can see Boole struggling to explain his realization that logic can be reduced to symbols and manipulated through mathematical operations. This was an incredibly bold proposition as can be inferred from some of Boole's quotes.

GUIDED PRACTICE

To demonstrate how Boolean logic works, you as the teacher are going to explore the different sets of students in the class using AND, OR, and NOT statements. Using a standard deck of playing cards that you have shuffled, pass out one card to each student in the class. Students will stand up or sit down as statements include or exclude their cards.

Boolean Example 1
 1. Stand up if your card is black OR red.
 2. Stay standing if your card is NOT red.
 3. Stay standing if your card has an even number AND is a club.

Review Standing Set: Clubs with even numbers

Boolean Example 2
1. Stand up if your card does NOT have a number.
2. Stand up if your card is an odd number AND is red.
3. Stay standing if (your card number is greater than 4 AND less than 8) OR (your card is a spade OR a diamond)

Review Standing Set: Spade and diamond face cards AND red number cards that are 5 or 7

You can create additional example sets as needed to increase or decrease the complexity. If you have a projector, it might help to show the text for the statements, especially as complexity increases and parenthetical items are introduced.

Read and Discuss

Have students reread each section of the text and discuss the following:
- Why do computers need Boolean logic?
- Why was George Boole's development of logic as a mathematical system so incredible?
- What aspects of computer programming can be seen in Boole's writing?
- How does AND work? OR? NOT?
- Which operations limit a set and which expand it?
- How do parentheses impact a Boolean logic statement?

MODEL

Use the following scenarios to introduce how Boolean logic works within the mechanisms of Old Town. For each group of students, set up the game board with the pieces, but only use the cards specified to present brief examples of game play.

Scenario 1

Cards: 7, 9, 50

Starting from an empty game board, with the players having the printer's building and the prison in front of them as the possible "my buildings" for the scenario. Play card 7 [The printer's entrance was in Cemetery Rd.]. This will require placement of printer tokens on the four southern most building spaces as indicated on the card image. Then play card 9 [The prison was west of Dalton Rd.] and add prison tokens to the four western building spots as shown on the card. Now consider card 50. Card 50 states that "my building" is in either the northern or southern outskirts.

Looking at the current situation on the game board and comparing it to the locations depicted on the card, students should notice two critical points. First, playing this card using the variable of "my building" as the printer's doesn't make any sense. It doesn't further limit the information shown on the map and simply confirms that it could be any one of the four southern building spots. Thus, card 50 cannot be played at this time with the printer's as the variable. Now consider using the prison as the variable. The result is much different; suddenly the AND operation of combining the existing set and the new rule set results in only a single true result. Given the combination of card 9 and card 50, the prison must be located in the building in the southwest corner. That is the only building in the set of card 9 AND card 50.

Scenario 2

Cards: 1, 7, 31, 55

Start with an empty game board and the church and printer's buildings as the "my building" possibilities. Play the cards in numerical order: 1, 7, 31, and then 55. What is the result? In this case it depends on which variable the group decides to use as the "my building" for cards 31 and 55. Depending on the variable declaration, the final building placement will be different.

Independent Practice

Remind students of the vocabulary introduced for their reading and ask them to attempt to include that vocabulary in appropriate ways in the writing activities they do.

Writing Activities

Narrative: You want to locate a new business in Old Town. Choose your business, draw a map of your view of Old Town, place a few businesses on the map, then write five Boolean logic statements that will determine the location of your new business.

Inform or Explain: Explain the use of parentheses in Boolean logic statements to create more complex formulas.

Express an Opinion: When you are searching on Google using two or more keywords, Google automatically treats these as an OR statement. In what different situations might this be helpful or not? What do you think the best default for a search string would be?

Sharing/Reflection

Have individuals or groups share and discuss their work with the class.

Assessment

Collect completed formative assessment (activity for model section) and writing activities and review. The solutions for the second scenario can differ slightly depending on which business is selected for "my building" first. If the church is used for card 31, the drugstore will be next to it; otherwise, the drugstore will be next to the printer's. For the narrative, the key point to look for is that the five statements narrow down placement to result in only a single possible location without any of the statements being contradictory. In the opinion, points raised will likely vary greatly as this is a non-technical review of a very technical issue. However, main concepts to look for include the fact that AND limits results while OR greatly expands them.

EXTENSION ACTIVITIES

Further Research: Research logic gates, and create a presentation that shows the symbols for logic gates and provides examples of their application.

Important Details: Have students identify ten important details to know about Boolean logic and justify their choices of those details using the Important Details sheet in the appendix and available online at www.teachingthroughgames.com for printing. Answers will vary.

THE MATHEMATICAL ANALYSIS OF LOGIC

By George Boole, 1847. Excerpt from the introduction.

They who are acquainted with the present state of the theory of Symbolical Algebra, are aware, that the validity of the processes of analysis does not depend upon the interpretation of the symbols which are employed, but solely upon the laws of their combination. **Every system of interpretation which does not affect the truth of the relations supposed, is equally admissible, and it is thus that the same process may, under one scheme of interpretation, represent the solution of a question on the properties of numbers, under another, that of a geometrical problem, and under a third, that of a problem of dynamics or optics.** This principle is indeed of fundamental importance; and it may with safety be affirmed, that the recent advances of pure analysis have been much assisted by the influence which it has exerted in directing the current of investigation.

But the full recognition of the consequences of this important doctrine has been, in some measure, retarded by accidental circumstances. **It has happened in every known form of analysis, that the elements to be determined have been conceived as measurable by comparison with some fixed standard. The predominant idea has been that of magnitude, or more strictly, of numerical ratio. The expression of magnitude, or of operations upon magnitude, has been the express object for which the symbols of Analysis have been invented, and for which their laws have been investigated. Thus the abstractions of the modern Analysis, not less than the ostensive diagrams of the ancient Geometry, have encouraged the notion, that Mathematics are essentially, as well as actually, the Science of Magnitude.**

The consideration of that view which has already been stated, as embodying the true principle of the Algebra of Symbols, would, however, lead us to infer that this conclusion is by no means necessary. **If every existing interpretation is shown to involve the idea of magnitude, it is only by <u>induction</u> that we can assert that no other interpretation is possible.** And it may be doubted whether our experience is sufficient to render such an induction legitimate. The history of pure Analysis is, it may be said, too recent to permit us to set limits to the extent of its applications. Should we grant to the inference a high degree of probability, we might still, and with reason, maintain the sufficiency of the definition to which the principle already stated would lead us. We might justly assign it as the definitive character of a true Calculus, that it is a method resting upon the employment of Symbols, whose laws of combination are known and general, and whose results admit of a consistent interpretation. That to the existing forms of Analysis a quantitative interpretation is assigned, is the result of the circumstances by which those forms were determined, and is not to be construed into a universal condition of Analysis. **It is upon the foundation of this general principle, that I purpose to establish the <u>Calculus of Logic</u>, and that I claim for it a place among the acknowledged forms of Mathematical Analysis, regardless that in its object and in its instruments it must at present stand alone.**

That which renders Logic possible, is the existence in our minds of general notions,—our ability to conceive of a <u>class</u>, and to designate its individual members by a common name. The theory of Logic is thus intimately connected with that of Language. A successful attempt to express logical propositions by symbols, the laws of whose combinations should be founded upon the laws of the mental processes which they represent, would, so far, be a step toward a philosophical language. But this is a view which we need not here follow into detail. **Assuming the notion of a class, we are able, from any conceivable collection of objects, to separate by a mental act, those which belong to the given class, and to contemplate them apart from the rest.** Such, or a similar act of election, we may conceive to be repeated. **The group of individuals left under consideration may be still further limited, by mentally selecting those among them which belong to some other recognised class, as well as to the one before contemplated. And this process may be repeated with other elements of distinction, until we arrive at an individual possessing all the distinctive characters which we have taken into account, and a member, at the same time, of every class which we have enumerated.** It is in fact a method similar to this which we employ whenever, in common language, we accumulate descriptive epithets for the sake of more precise definition.

Now the several mental operations which in the above case we have supposed to be performed, are subject to peculiar laws. It is possible to assign relations among them, whether as respects the repetition of a given operation or the succession of different ones, or some other particular, which are never violated. **It is, for example, true that the result of two successive acts is unaffected by the order in which they are performed**; and there are at least two other laws which will be pointed out in the proper place. **These will perhaps to some appear so obvious as to be ranked among necessary truths, and so little important as to be undeserving of special notice. And probably they are noticed for the first time in this Essay. Yet it may with confidence be asserted, that if they were** other than they are, the entire mechanism of reasoning, nay the very laws and constitution of the human intellect, would be vitally changed. A Logic might indeed exist, but it would no longer be the Logic we possess.

Such are the elementary laws upon the existence of which, and upon their capability of exact symbolical expression, the method of the following Essay is founded; and it is presumed that the object which it seeks to attain will be thought to have been very fully accomplished. **Every logical proposition, whether categorical or hypothetical, will be found to be capable of exact and rigorous expression, and not only will the laws of conversion and of syllogism be thence deducible, but the resolution of the most complex systems of propositions, the separation of any proposed element, and the expression of its value in terms of the remaining elements, with every subsidiary relation involved.** Every process will represent <u>deduction</u>, every mathematical consequence will express a logical <u>inference</u>. The generality of the method will even permit us to express arbitrary operations of the intellect, and thus lead to the demonstration of general theorems in logic analogous, in no slight degree, to the general theorems of ordinary mathematics. No inconsiderable part of the pleasure which we derive from the application of analysis to the interpretation of external nature, arises from the conceptions which it enables us to form of the universality of the dominion of law. The general formulae to which we are conducted seem to give to that element a visible presence, and the multitude of particular cases to which they apply, demonstrate the extent of its sway. Even the symmetry of their analytical expression may in no fanciful sense be deemed indicative of its harmony and its consistency. Now I do not presume to say to what extent the same sources of pleasure are opened in the following Essay. The measure of that extent may be left to the estimate of those who shall think the subject worthy of their study. But I may venture to assert that such occasions of intellectual gratification are not here wanting. **The laws we have to examine are the laws of one of the most important of our mental faculties. The mathematics we have to construct are**

the mathematics of the human intellect. Nor are the form and character of the method, apart from all regard to its interpretation, undeserving of notice. There is even a remarkable exemplification, in its general theorems, of that species of excellence which consists in freedom from exception. And this is observed where, in the corresponding cases of the received mathematics, such a character is by no means apparent. The few who think that there is that in analysis which renders it deserving of attention for its own sake, may find it worth while to study it under a form in which every equation can be solved and every solution interpreted. Nor will it lessen the interest of this study to reflect that every peculiarity which they will notice in the form of the Calculus represents a corresponding feature in the constitution of their own minds.

°°°

The relation in which this Essay stands at once to Logic and to Mathematics, may further justify some notice of the question which has lately been revived, as to the relative value of the two studies in a liberal education. One of the chief objections which 'have been urged against the study of Mathematics in general, is but another form of that which has been already considered with respect to the use of symbols in particular. And it need not here be further dwelt upon, than to notice, that if it avails anything, it applies with an equal force against the study of Logic. The canonical forms of the Aristotelian syllogism are really symbolical; only the symbols are less perfect of their kind than those of mathematics. If they are employed to test the validity of an argument, they as truly supersede the exercise of reason, as does a reference to a formula of analysis. Whether men do, in the present day, make this use of the Aristotelian canons, except as a special illustration of the rules of Logic, may be doubted; yet it cannot be questioned that when the authority of Aristotle was dominant in the schools of Europe, such applications were habitually made. And our argument only requires the admission, that the case is possible.

But the question before us has been argued upon higher grounds. Regarding Logic as a branch of Philosophy, and defining Philosophy as the "science of a real existence," and "the research of causes," and assigning as its main business the investigation of the "why," while Mathematics display only the "that." **Sir W. Hamilton has contended, not simply, that the superiority rests with the study of Logic, but that the study of Mathematics is at once dangerous and useless. The pursuits of the mathematician "have not only not trained him to that acute scent, to that delicate, almost instinctive, tact which, in the <u>twilight of probability</u>, the search and discrimination of its finer facts demand; they have gone to cloud his vision, to <u>indurate</u> his touch, to all but the blazing light, the iron chain of demonstration, and left him out of the narrow confines of his science, to a passive credulity in any premises, or to an absolute incredulity in all."** In support of these and of other charges, both argument and copious authority are adduced. I shall not attempt a complete discussion of the topics which are suggested by these remarks. My object is not controversy, and the observations which follow are offered not in the spirit of antagonism, but in the hope of contributing to the formation of just views upon an important subject. Of Sir W. Hamilton it is impossible to speak otherwise than with that respect which is due to genius and learning.

Philosophy is then described as the science of a real existence and the research of causes. And that no doubt may rest upon the meaning of the word cause, it is further said, that philosophy "mainly investigates the why." These definitions are common among the ancient writers. Thus Seneca, one of Sir W. Hamilton's authorities, Epistle LXXXVIII., "The philosopher seeks and knows the causes of natural things, of which the mathematician searches out and computes the numbers and the measures." It may be remarked, in passing, that in whatever degree the belief has prevailed, that the business of philosophy is immediately with causes; in the same degree has every science whose object is the investigation of laws, been lightly esteemed. Thus the Epistle to which we have referred, bestows, by contrast with Philosophy, a separate condemnation on Music and Grammar, on Mathematics and Astronomy, although it is that of Mathematics only that Sir W. Hamilton has quoted.

Now we might take our stand upon the conviction of many thoughtful and reflective minds, that in the extent of the meaning above stated, Philosophy is impossible. The business of true Science, they conclude, is with laws and phenomena. The nature of Being, the mode of the operation of Cause, the why, they hold to be beyond the reach of our intelligence. But we do not require the vantage-ground of this position; nor is it doubted that whether the aim of Philosophy is attainable or not, the desire which impels us to the attempt is an instinct of our higher nature. Let it be granted that the problem which has baffled the efforts of ages, is not a hopeless one; that the "science of a real existence," and " the research of causes," "that kernel" for which "Philosophy is still militant," do not transcend the limits of the human intellect. **I am then compelled to assert, that according to this view of the nature of Philosophy, Logic forms no part of it. On the principle of a true classification, we ought no longer to associate Logic and Metaphysics, but Logic and Mathematics.**

Should any one after what has been said, entertain a doubt upon this point, I must refer him to the evidence which will be afforded in the following Essay. **He will there see Logic resting like Geometry upon axiomatic truths, and its theorems constructed upon that general doctrine of symbols, which constitutes the foundation of the recognised Analysis. In the Logic of Aristotle he will be led to view a collection of the formulae of the science, expressed by another, but, (it is thought) less perfect scheme of symbols.** I feel bound to contend for the absolute exactness of this parallel. It is no escape from the conclusion to which it points to assert, that Logic not only constructs a science, but also inquires into the origin and the nature of its own principles,—a distinction which is denied to Mathematics. "It is wholly beyond the domain of mathematicians," it is said, "to inquire into the origin and nature of their principles."— Review, page 415. But upon what ground can such a distinction be maintained? What definition of the term Science will be found sufficiently arbitrary to allow such differences?

The application of this conclusion to the question before us is clear and decisive. The mental discipline which is afforded by

the study of Logic, as an exact science, is, in species, the same as that afforded by the study of Analysis.

Is it then contended that either Logic or Mathematics can supply a perfect discipline to the Intellect? The most careful and unprejudiced examination of this question leads me to doubt whether such a position can be maintained. The exclusive claims of either must, I believe, be abandoned, nor can any others, partaking of a like exclusive character, be admitted in their room. **It is an important observation, which has more than once been made, that it is one thing to arrive at correct premises, and another thing to deduce logical conclusions, and that the business of life depends more upon the former than upon the latter. The study of the exact sciences may teach us the one, and it may give us some general preparation of knowledge and of practice for the attainment of the other, but it is to the union of thought with action, in the field of Practical Logic, the arena of Human Life, that we are to look for its fuller and more perfect accomplishment.**

I desire here to express my conviction, that **with the advance of our knowledge of all true science, an ever-increasing harmony will be found to prevail among its separate branches.** The view which leads to the rejection of one, ought, if consistent, to lead to the rejection of others. And indeed many of the authorities which have been quoted against the study of Mathematics, are even more explicit in their condemnation of Logic. "Natural science," says the Chian Aristo, " is above us, Logical science does not concern us." When such conclusions are founded (as they ofien are) upon a deep conviction of the preeminent value and importance of the study of Morals, we admit the premises, but must demur to the inference. **For it has been well said by an ancient writer, that it is the "characteristic of the liberal sciences, not that they conduct us to Virtue, but that they prepare us for Virtue;"** and Melancthon's sentiment, "**abeunt studia in mores**," has passed into a proverb. Moreover, there is a common ground upon which all sincere votaries of truth may meet, exchanging with each other the language of Flamstecd's appeal to Newton, "The works of the Eternal Providence will be better understood through your labors and mine."

LESSON PLAN 3B

ESSENTIAL QUESTION

Is the concept of "true" in Boolean logic absolute?

VOCABULARY

The following vocabulary words are important concepts for the content of this lesson.
- Absolute truth
- XAND
- XOR
- NAND
- NOR
- XNOR

MINI READING LESSON

While you are discussing logic and working through the exercises, attempt to answer the following question: How is truth in Boolean logic situational rather than absolute? Introduce the vocabulary words above. They can be introduced even if they are not in the specific reading you have chosen.

GUIDED PRACTICE

Remind students of the scenarios from the previous lesson. Demonstrate the situational truth of Boolean logic using this third scenario.

Scenario 3

Cards: 7, 53

When card 7 is played, it places four potential tokens for the printer's shop in the four southern most building spots. In this situation, however, card 53 cannot be played using the printer's shop as the variable. It cannot be true as there is no overlap in the possible building sites. Remind students that as they play Old Town, there will be many such cards that, given the situation on the board, cannot be true and thus cannot be played. If you have two cards in hand that cannot be played—either because they cannot be true, or because they add no new information to the board—the two cards can be discarded and one potential token can be removed from the board and scored as a point. This can be a very powerful move later in the game.

Have students preview any headings and subheadings in the reading they have been asked to do. Have students read the selections.

Read and Discuss

Have students reread each section of the text and discuss the following:
- How does "true" in Boolean logic differ from the "truth"?
- How are more complex Boolean operations like XOR or NAND examples of computer efficiency?
- Give an example of when you would use XOR in your daily life.

MODEL

Play Old Town using the full rule set. The game is designed for up to four players, but it can be modified to play with teams. This is a challenging game that requires a very high level of abstract thinking, and so having teammates to talk with can help students do the needed processing. For assessment, you as the teacher should listen to teams talking through situations in the game. Or, if Old Town is being played by individuals, have them keep a log of their thinking process.

INDEPENDENT PRACTICE

Remind students of the vocabulary introduced for their reading and ask them to attempt to include that vocabulary in appropriate ways in the writing activities they do.

Writing Activities

Inform or Explain: Create a logic gate system that will help someone select types of clothes to wear. For example, checking between shorts or pants would use an XOR gate; one would not wear shorts AND pants. Students should think of at least ten checks that would happen using a variety of different basic and advanced logic gates.

Express an Opinion: Was Old Town an easy game to play? Why or why not?

SHARING/REFLECTION

Have individuals or groups share and discuss their work with the class.

ASSESSMENT

Collect completed formative assessment (activity for Model section) and writing activities and review or think back to your observations as teams played the game. For the inform piece, students should properly use the logic gates to make meaningful selections. For the opinion piece, the answer is obviously quite personal. Positions should be backed by some evidence and supporting statements, though.

EXTENSION ACTIVITIES

Further Play: Download Minecraft and explore available online tutorials that explain how to build logic gates within the game.

Further Research: Explore additional search operators available in search engines like Google or Bing. How do they go beyond the basic Boolean operators or rework them to make the concepts easier to understand and use? Produce a one-page tutorial sheet that can help others understand how to make efficient use of advanced search options.

Timeline: Create a series of timelines showing major points or key figures in areas such as computer hardware, software, and programming languages.

GAME 4:
PARSELY SYSTEM

I n the days before color monitors and games with lifelike graphics, people spent many hours exploring interactive text games. In the 1970s and 1980s this type of game used well-written text to evoke imagery in the minds of players. As a comparison, the "graphical" games of the period included a genre of games called roguelike— named for a game called *Rogue* introduced in 1980. These dungeon crawling games were built using ASCII graphics; the walls, floor, and monsters were all made from text characters. The *Diablo* series is actually just a very graphical implementation of a roguelike game. This section, however, explores the world of games without even rudimentary ASCII graphics—games that you can and will be programming in the upcoming lessons using the Parsely Game System (Momento Mori) and a human filling in as the computer program.

TECHNICALLY SPEAKING

GAMING BEFORE GRAPHICS

Today, the genre under discussion is most often referred to as interactive fiction or interactive text as a nod to its format more reminiscent of a book than what we might think of as a modern computer game. In earlier days, though, the genre was more often called text-based adventure games. As with the naming of the roguelike genre, text-based adventure games can be traced back to *Colossal Cave Adventure* designed by Will Crowther in 1975. One of the most famous of the text-based adventures that followed was *Zork*, written in 1977 by some students at MIT. The game was widely distributed on ARPANET, established by the U.S. Department of Defense as a national network that predates the modern Internet.

In 1978, Roy Trubshaw at Essex University in the United Kingdom developed a multi-user dungeon game that, when Essex University joined ARPANET in 1980, became the first online multiplayer role-playing game. *World of Warcraft* can be traced directly back to the interactive fiction genre of games that we are going to write. *WoW* has millions of players today, but its origins can be traced back to the humble text adventure games of the 1970s that used a basic computer parser to interpret and react to textual commands.

How Interactive Text Works

As a computer program, interactive text games use a simple computer parser to interpret, or parse, text commands entered by the player that will then cause changes in the text. For example, if a player enters the command to "go west," the program will then modify the text to write out the "page" for the room to the west of the current player position. The computer parsed the command to understand what the player wanted to happen. The verb "go" is an established command verb, and the direction "west" that follows would have been an established exit connecting the first room to the second room. The variability of language—go, amble, walk, stroll, proceed—means that the programmer either has to establish a list of allowed commands or create a thesaurus to help the computer understand that all of those words mean "go". The nouns within commands are usually established in the written description for the room where the player is. Descriptions have to be carefully written to provide clues for the reader/player as to which objects are programmed to be interactive.

Normally, the parser within the computer program running the interactive text game handles all of this behind the scenes. Inform 7 is a modern interactive text program that makes writing and playing games very easy. Using the Parsely Game System, though, we can create an analog version of the computer program in which a person fills in the role of computer parser. The system provides a realistic introduction to coding concepts and principles without the layers of technology. Students have to think like computer programmers writing code. They are still constrained by language, logical connections, and consistencies within both the narrative and the program. With the Parsely Game System, though, there are no computers involved. Simple paper and pencil allows for the creation of robust and complex playable interactive text games.

Writing Interactive Texts

Writing computer programs is actually a very complex writing task. Instead of addressing a single reading audience, computer programmers have to write for two very different audiences. On a technical level, they have to write the program code for the computer that is going to execute the commands. They also have to write the interactive elements for the end user who is going to experience the program. This idea of audience is not a technology concept, but actually one that comes from writing. Writers need to be very aware of who their audience is, tailoring language choice, writing style, complexity, and a host of other elements to the target audience. In interactive text games, the author has to write both a story that unfolds as the player explores the world and solves problems to progress forward. Characters, settings, plot devices, and all the other story elements have to be created. Added to this, though, is the game level of programmatic writing that describes the interface, movement, and the way in which the end user discovers hidden elements.

Traditional stories are very controlled in how they unfold. The writer dictates the flow of the story—when characters enter rooms and encounter people. In games, especially more contemporary games, that environment is more fluid and open. Game designers need to include triggers or logical cause and effect actions—i.e., if-then(-else) and other conditional statements—that advance the reader to the next stage of the story. The identification of logical situations and anticipating the actions of the end user and how they will attempt to control the program are at the heart of the user experience aspects of programming.

In a traditional story, an author may describe how a character enters a room, hears a noise, discovers the noise is coming from the next room, searches and finds the key hidden under the pillow, and enters the next room to find a rat. In a game environment, it is often up the user to decide if or when to explore the noise. While the designer can include the elements in a linear way, forcing the players to engage with the elements in order, this can make for a less engaging game design. Good design puts choice, decision, and problem solving in the hands of the players. Better game design will also include well-written interactive text with hints and prompts. If you need players to do something, provide enough clues to make sure they understand what they should be doing.

In many computer games, the concept of choice is often just an illusion. The mechanisms behind the game require a linear progression of plot elements to proceed. The mechanisms seem to provide choice to the player and variation to how the experience unfolds, but in the end the code dictates that certain actions must be completed to move forward. In the previous example, the players need to find the key before they can gain entrance to the room and find the rat. The designer chooses how difficult it is to find the key, or perhaps they can build in a secondary way to gain entrance to the room, giving more options for the players. What might happen, for example, if the player tried to break down the door? If there is no computer code to handle this situation, nothing will happen.

WRITING IN THE PARSELY SYSTEM

The Parsely System provides a pen and pencil opportunity for students to begin to practice writing interactive texts as a type of rudimentary computer programming. Students will need to create a story or nonfiction narrative and then structure it within the code of the Parsely System. This means that they will need to describe the basic elements of a "room" within interactive text.

Rooms

A room is a location—any location, not just what we think of as a room usually—in an interactive text game. Rooms have descriptions that are shared when a player enters the room.

Parking Lot: You are standing in a large parking lot outside of the school.

Exits

Rooms are connected together through exits. Exits are shared with players at the end of a room description to let them know which directions they can move to find a new room. Sometimes exits are hidden or locked.

Parking Lot: You are standing in a large parking lot outside of the school. The main doors for the school are in front of you. Exits are: in.

Items

To introduce plot devices or provide additional description within the scenery of a room, writers can introduce items. As with object-oriented programming, modern interactive text programs like Inform 7 use classes for items. For example, some items are "supporters," meaning other items can be placed on top of them, while others are "containers" that can hold additional items. This makes creating a table or bag faster as the properties of a supporter or container are already established. Items should have additional descriptions provided if they are important to help players figure out what to do after looking at or examining the item.

Parking Lot: You are standing in a large parking lot outside of the high school surrounded by trees. Your beat-up old car is parked amongst the many other cars in the student section of the lot. The main doors for the school jut out from the main building. Exits are: in.

Actions

In addition to writing the narrative text portions seen in the examples above, an author writing in the Parsely System also has to establish programmatic responses for player actions. These are written as a response to parsed commands typically consisting of a verb and noun acting as a predicate and a subject.

Examine Car: There are many cars here, but your eyes are drawn to the dents and dings that make your blue sedan so familiar. The trunk is ajar from where you released it before exiting the car.
Open Trunk: You open up the trunk of your car to see your backpack and a bottle of water.
Take Backpack: You pick up the backpack and sling it across one shoulder.

In the following lessons, you will begin writing analog computer programs using the Parsely System. Think carefully as you write your code about the two audiences and the need to anticipate and define points of interaction. Being analog with a human serving as the parser, the Parsely System can be much more forgiving of omissions; experienced facilitators will interpret and enhance responses based on what you write, but don't rely on this.

LESSON PLAN 4A

ESSENTIAL QUESTION

When does a story become a game?

VOCABULARY

The following vocabulary words are important concepts for the content of this lesson.:
- Interactive text
- Text adventure
- Parser
- Command
- Parsely System

MINI READING LESSON

While you are discussing interactive text and playing the games, attempt to answer the following question: What changes do we need to make to turn a story into an interactive game? Introduce the previous vocabulary words. They can be introduced even if they are not in the specific reading you have chosen.

GUIDED PRACTICE

To introduce Parsely games, you as the teacher are going to serve as the parser for the micro-game, Flaming Goat. This game is found on the Action Castle II game board. Explain that micro-games are very small interactions that typically have only a couple of rooms and about five to ten steps needed to solve the problem. The games work by having players give the parser a single brief command consisting of a predicate and a subject. For example: examine desk, go out, take pen. As the parser, you will be able to adjust the level of difficulty as appropriate, but for the highest level of understanding it is suggested that you be extremely literal. This mirrors the peanut butter sandwich activity in section 1. Then, play through Flaming Goat.

Have students preview any headings and subheadings in the reading they have been asked to do. Have students read the selections.

Read and Discuss

Have students reread each section of the text and discuss the following:
- How did interactions with the parser in Flaming Goat compare with playing other games?
- Is the parser more or less restrictive than a graphical game?
- How difficult was it to follow the game in your head?

MODEL

Have the students work together in small groups to map out the steps needed to solve the problem in Flaming Goat. 1) examine machine, 2) take soda, 3) go up, 4) open soda, 5) pour on goat, 6) feed goat can, 7) go on to work. Students should then work within the groups to design a micro-game with up to two rooms and up to ten problem steps. Have each group identify a member that will serve as the parser to run the games for the whole class. When the parsers are identified, switch the games around so they are running a game from a different group. This will show whether or not the game has enough information provided. Finish by having students reflect on the design process and the challenges they faced during the design process.

INDEPENDENT PRACTICE

Remind students of the vocabulary introduced for their reading and ask them to attempt to include that vocabulary in appropriate ways in the writing activities they do.

Writing Activities

Narrative: Select a well-known fairy tale or short story like "Little Red Riding Hood." Pick one section from the story (one room, no more than five steps) and write it as an interactive text game.

Inform or Explain: Think of a well-known book. What changes would have to be made to create an interactive text from that book? Describe at least five changes.

SHARING/REFLECTION

Have individuals or groups share and discuss their work with the class.

ASSESSMENT

Collect completed formative assessment (activity for model section) and writing activities and review. The reflection from the game experience should include information about how the game might need to be changed based on play testing. For the narrative piece, students should demonstrate understanding of the Parsely System of writing. In the inform piece, answers should touch on concepts like the diminished role of dialogue, the need to condense setting, the need to promote actions, and the challenge of creating choices and problems to be solved.

EXTENSION ACTIVITIES

Further Play: Have students serve as a parser running a Parsely System micro-game for friends or family. Write a reflective piece that describes their experience and feedback from the players.

Important Details: Have students identify ten important details to know and justify their choices of those details using the Important Details sheet in the appendix and available online at www.teachingthroughgames.com for printing. Answers will vary.

LESSON PLAN 4B

ESSENTIAL QUESTION

How do designers create engagement when creating interactive media?

VOCABULARY

The following vocabulary words are important concepts for the content of this lesson:

- Interactive media
- Decision point
- Discoverable elements
- Logical chain

MINI READING LESSON

While you are discussing interactive text and playing the games, attempt to answer the following question: What strategies and design practices can make interactive media–like games more engaging? Introduce the previous vocabulary words. They can be introduced even if they are not in the specific reading you have chosen.

GUIDED PRACTICE

Describe for students the difference between interactive media–like games and passive media like television. Interactive text games combine stories with interactive game elements. In the last lesson students experienced a micro-game. Now, lead them through the larger Action Castle II game serving as the parser. This is a more complex game with seventeen rooms and a much more detailed problem to solve. It requires more effort from both the parser and the players who will have to track progress in their heads. The game sheet does include a map for the parser to follow. For initial work with students, it may help to show the map or have someone drawing a map as they explore the world. After the students play the game, talk about the difference between newer computer games that automatically record information to a quest log and map every place you visit compared to interactive text games where the player has to complete these tasks.

Have students preview any headings and subheadings in the reading they have been asked to do. Have students read the selections.

Read and Discuss

Have students reread each section of the text and think about the game experience to discuss the following:
- Does having to track progress through the game in your head or using hand-drawn maps and notes make the game more or less engaging?
- How did the author of Action Castle prompt you as a player to take certain desired actions?
- Did you notice the work being done by the parser? Teacher: you may need to prompt discussion here or provide

examples. For instance, in the Old Pond Road room, did players give a look sign command where you had to add in a prompt to get them to issue the read sign command?

- The goal was not defined at the start of the game. Would you have liked to have known the goal at the beginning?

MODEL

In small groups, have students play through Action Castle II or another longer game in the Parsely System to have them gain additional experience serving as a parser and reading the code for the game. Prompt students to think carefully about any instances where they have to add additional code to the written program. Let them know that they will be writing about their experience with the code, so if they need to take quick notes to help them remember situations that might be good. After the play experience, have students write a reflection on the nature and quality of the code within the program for the game they ran. How much did they as a human have to add to the code? At what points would the game experience have failed if a computer had been parsing it?

INDEPENDENT PRACTICE

Remind students of the vocabulary introduced for their reading and ask them to attempt to include that vocabulary in appropriate ways in the writing activities they do.

Writing Activities

Narrative: Write a narrative about how the experience of running the Parsely game for the group would have gone differently had you been acting as a robot. How might the players have felt and reacted?

Inform or Explain: Programming is an exact and explicit writing style. Explain how writing a computer program is similar to writing a recipe that a novice cook will follow exactly as written.

Express an Opinion: Can interactive text games ever be as engaging as *World of Warcraft* or a similarly graphic game? Defend your answer.

SHARING/REFLECTION

Have individuals or groups share and discuss their work with the class.

ASSESSMENT

Collect completed formative assessment (activity for model section) and writing activities and review. The reflection from the model section should include at least some examples of instances where the parser had to use human interpretation. The style for Parsely writing means that this is an expectation. For the narrative piece, it would be expected that players facing a robotic parser interpretation would feel frustration. Having to guess a verb or solve a puzzle with limited or no prompts is very hard. In the opinion piece, answers will probably be a resounding no. We are so used to highly graphical video games, that sometimes the quality of a story is overlooked because of all the flashy movement.

EXTENSION ACTIVITIES

Further Research: Explore the Inform 7 interactive fiction language at http://inform7.com. Inform 7 uses a very simple language system for coding interactive text games in natural language, i.e. plain English. Explore the source code for games to read the programing language, and try programming a short interactive text game yourself.

Further Writing: Though it is often called interactive fiction, we have been calling the genre interactive texts to be more inclusive.

Try creating an interactive nonfiction game based on history or science. How might the solar system or the settlement of the United States be depicted in an interactive text?

APPENDIX 1
CURRICULUM ALIGNMENTS
COMMON CORE LEARNING STANDARDS

The following concepts from the Common Core State Standards are addressed in this unit:

READING INFORMATIONAL TEXTS RELATED TO GRADE 6–8 STANDARDS

- Cite specific textual evidence to support analysis of primary and secondary sources.
- Determine the central ideas or information of a primary or secondary source; provide an accurate summary of the source distinct from prior knowledge or opinions.
- Identify key steps in a text's description of a process related to history/social studies (e.g., how a bill becomes law, how interest rates are raised or lowered).
- Determine the meaning of words and phrases as they are used in a text, including vocabulary specific to domains related to history/social studies.
- Describe how a text presents information (e.g., sequentially, comparatively, causally).
- Identify aspects of a text that reveal an author's point of view or purpose (e.g., loaded language, inclusion or avoidance of particular facts).
- Integrate visual information (e.g., in charts, graphs, photographs, videos, or maps) with other information in print and digital texts.
- Distinguish among fact, opinion, and reasoned judgment in a text.
- Analyze the relationship between a primary and secondary source on the same topic.

Writing Standards Related to Grade 6–8 Standards

- Write arguments to support claims with clear reasons and relevant evidence.
- Write informative/explanatory texts to examine a topic and convey ideas, concepts, and information through the selection, organization, and analysis of relevant content.
- Write narratives to develop real or imagined experiences or events using effective technique, relevant descriptive details, and well-structured event sequences.
- Conduct short research projects to answer a question, drawing on several sources and refocusing the inquiry when appropriate.
- Gather relevant information from multiple print and digital sources; assess the credibility of each source; and quote or paraphrase the data and conclusions of others while avoiding plagiarism and providing basic bibliographic information for sources.
- Draw evidence from literary or informational texts to support analysis, reflection, and research.

Reading Informational Texts Related to Grade 9–12 Standards

- CCSS.ELA-LITERACY.RI.9-10.1
  Cite strong and thorough textual evidence to support analysis of what the text says explicitly as well as inferences drawn from the text.
- CCSS.ELA-LITERACY.RI.9-10.5
  Analyze in detail how an author's ideas or claims are developed and refined by particular sentences, paragraphs, or larger portions of a text (e.g., a section or chapter).
- CCSS.ELA-LITERACY.RI.11-12.1
  Cite strong and thorough textual evidence to support analysis of what the text says explicitly as well as inferences drawn from the text, including determining where the text leaves matters uncertain.

- CCSS.ELA-LITERACY.RI.11-12.7
Integrate and evaluate multiple sources of information presented in different media or formats (e.g., visually, quantitatively) as well as in words in order to address a question or solve a problem.

Writing Standards Related to Grade 9–12 Standards

- CCSS.ELA-LITERACY.W.9-10.1 and CCSS. ELA-LITERACY.W.11-12.1
Write arguments to support claims in an analysis of substantive topics or texts, using valid reasoning and relevant and sufficient evidence.
- CCSS.ELA-LITERACY.W.9-10.2 and CCSS. ELA-LITERACY.W.11-12.2
Write informative/explanatory texts to examine and convey complex ideas, concepts, and information clearly and accurately through the effective selection, organization, and analysis of content.
- CCSS.ELA-LITERACY.W.9-10.3 and CCSS. ELA-LITERACY.W.11-12.3
Write narratives to develop real or imagined experiences or events using effective technique, well-chosen details, and well-structured event sequences.
- CCSS.ELA-LITERACY.W.9-10.6
Use technology, including the Internet, to produce, publish, and update individual or shared writing products, taking advantage of technology's capacity to link to other information and to display information flexibly and dynamically.
- CCSS.ELA-LITERACY.W.9-10.7 and CCSS. ELA-LITERACY.W.11-12.7
Conduct short as well as more sustained research projects to answer a question (including a self-generated question) or solve a problem; narrow or broaden the inquiry when appropriate;

synthesize multiple sources on the subject, demonstrating understanding of the subject under investigation.

- CCSS.ELA-LITERACY.W.9-10.8
Gather relevant information from multiple authoritative print and digital sources, using advanced searches effectively; assess the usefulness of each source in answering the research question; integrate information into the text selectively to maintain the flow of ideas, avoiding plagiarism and following a standard format for citation.

- CCSS.ELA-LITERACY.W.11-12.8
Gather relevant information from multiple authoritative print and digital sources, using advanced searches effectively; assess the strengths and limitations of each source in terms of the task, purpose, and audience; integrate information into the text selectively to maintain the flow of ideas, avoiding plagiarism and overreliance on any one source and following a standard format for citation.

- CCSS.ELA-LITERACY.W.9-10.9 and CCSS.ELA-LITERACY.W.11-12.9
Draw evidence from literary or informational texts to support analysis, reflection, and research.

Technology Standards Related to Grade 6–12 Standards

Standards from: http://www.iste.org/docs/pdfs/20-14_ISTE_Standards-S_PDF.pdf

This technology resourse seeks to encourage students to explore the underlying thinking about technology operations and concepts and so relates to the International Society for Technology in Education on operations and concepts which follows.

6. Technology operations and concepts

Students demonstrate a sound understanding of technology concepts, systems, and operations.

a. Understand and use technology systems
b. Select and use applications effectively and productively
c. Troubleshoot systems and applications
d. Transfer current knowledge to learning of new technologies

This work relates most closely to parts a, c, and d of the standard. This work, however, addresses the foundation work required to implement this standard. It helps students understand how computers "think" and the requirements of any language a computer "uses." It helps students to understand technology systems, requires them to troubleshoot communication with a system, and allows for transfer of their acquired thinking skills to new systems.

APPENDIX 2

To access supplementary materials, go to http://www.teachingth-roughgames.com. Then enter the code word **thinksmart** in order to be directed to the following worksheets:"

RoboRally Planning Worksheet

Important Details Worksheet

Name:

Date:

RoboRally Planning Sheet

Use the arrow shapes and notations below to plan your path through the Risky Exchange map in RoboRally. Assume that you are starting on the board in the open space at the end of the single conveyer belt next to the double conveyer belt. From there, plan movements to direct your robot to visit each of the three waypoints as shown in the rules. Don't forget that after each of your movements, the conveyer belts will move and the spinners will rotate!

Rotate Left	Rotate Right	U-Turn	Move 1	Move 2	Move 3	Back Up
Rotate your robot 90° left	Rotate your robot 90° right	Rotate your robot 180°	Move your robot forward 1 space	Move your robot forward 2 spaces	Move your robot forward 3 spaces	Move your robot back 1 space

Record one arrow (and speed if required) using the available commands shown above

1	2	3	4	5	6	7	8	9	10	11	12	13	14	15
16	17	18	19	20	21	22	23	24	25	26	27	28	29	30
31	32	33	34	35	36	37	38	39	40	41	42	43	44	45
46	47	48	49	50	51	52	53	54	55	56	57	58	59	60
61	62	63	64	65	66	67	68	69	70	71	72	73	74	75
76	77	78	79	80	81	82	83	84	85	86	87	88	89	90
91	92	93	94	95	96	97	98	99	100	101	102	103	104	105

Rosen Classroom
PROFESSIONAL RESOURCES

	Important Detail	Reason Chosen
1		
2		
3		
4		
5		
6		
7		
8		
9		
10		

ABOUT THE AUTHORS

Christopher Harris, Editorial Director chris@playplaylearn.com Chris is the director of a School Library System in western New York that has provided a curriculum aligned board game library to member school districts since 2007. His current position as a certified school administrator, along with his background as a teacher, technology coordinator, and school librarian have provided Chris with many different perspectives on gaming and learning. Being able to speak with fellow administrators including principals and curriculum directors about the value of board games as a part of teaching and learning has been key to the success of the game library he founded as part of the Genesee Valley Educational Partnership School Library System in 2007. Chris was a member of the National Expert Panel for the American Library Association Gaming and Libraries grant in 2007-2008 and has continued to present nationally on gaming in schools and libraries as well as other school, technology and library topics. He writes a monthly column in School Library Journal called "The Next Big Thing" and co-authored *Libraries Got Game: Aligned Learning through Modern Board Games* (ALA Editions, 2010) with Brian Mayer.

Brian Mayer, Design & Development brian@playplaylearn.com A certified teacher and school librarian, Brian currently works as a gaming and library technology specialist for the Genesee Valley Educational Partnership where, since 2007, he has curated and managed a game library of over 300 curricularly aligned resources. Working with school librarians and classroom teachers, Brian utilizes game resources, design exercises and play experiences to help students engage with and find new meaning within the classroom curriculum. Brian is a founding board member of American Library Association's Games and Gaming Roundtable. Brian is the co-author of *Libraries Got Game: Aligned Learning through Modern Board Games* (ALA Editions, 2010). He has also written articles about gaming in schools and libraries for School Library Journal and Knowledge Quest, and presents and runs workshops at state and national conferences exploring the value of games and play for education and growth. In addition to this work, Brian is also the author of the game *Freedom: The Underground Railroad*, published by Academy Games in 2013. Freedom has gone on to win multiple awards and receive much critical acclaim.

Dr. Patricia Harris, Curriculum & Instruction pat@playplay-learn.com After working more than 10 years in public schools both rural and urban and spending 8 years at an engineering school teaching social sciences, communication skills, and technology, Dr. Patricia Harris spent the last years of her career as head of an elementary education program, technology coordinator for the education department, and educational consultant for a physicians assistant graduate program. Her research and practical focus in education has been working with teachers at all grade levels, including working with an elementary teacher to co-teach a clinical class for several years, to build pedagogical strength. Dr. Harris's experience with social studies and science instructional methodology helps inform the curriculum alignment and classroom use scenarios presented here.

NOTES

NOTES

NOTES